WARRIOR ANGEL

By

Dave Goodwin

Dedicated to my beautiful Toni.

For Toni

Lord I thank you for the times I have spent with Toni
Who came into my life
At my darkest hour
A breath of fresh air
A gentle breeze with immense power

There's something running through me
I don't know what
Feels like a warm glow
Turning cold to hot

With every conversation
I seem to get a lift
Whatever it is you're giving me
It's a wonderful gift

I find my demeanour changing
Like a power building within
Your words are igniting hope in me
That a new life can begin

My hope is getting stronger
Now belief is coming through
I'm changing as a person
All because of you

Downtrodden, beaten, defeated
Wallowing on my knees
Until you took my hand
And lifted me with ease

Now I can carry on
And live a life so true
The love I have in my heart
Is all because of you

I know that you'll stand with me
If I should fall again
Hope, belief and love within me
Will pull me through
Amen.

CONTENTS

Foreword

Well, a lot has happened this past year. I've still got all the ailments I had in my previous foreword. Heart monitor still inside my chest (although it doesn't work now, but due to Covid hasn't been removed).

Brain damage permanent, arthritis getting progressively worse, diabetes now stage one and I have to inject myself twice a day. All the other crap still affecting me on a regular basis. Blackouts still intermittent and apparently for no specific reason; they're like my nightmares and flashbacks, they just come without warning and usually at the most awkward or inconvenient times.

But the thing that almost destroyed me is the fact that my beautiful Toni is terminal with cancer. FFS, she's only in her forties. I would swap places with her right now if I could.

I wrote my first poetry book (*One Hundred Kisses for Toni*) to get a date with her. I think everyone knows the story by now. So this will be my last poetry book (apart from the revised edition of *Demons of the Mind but a Light Still Shines*). I think it's fitting, that I do this as a tribute to my beautiful Toni. *Warrior Angel* (and I chose the title because of the brilliant fight Toni has put up to stay with us) is a book of a variety of poems but is also my way of saying goodbye to the woman that really did save my life on a number of occasions and made sure I have the inner strength and willpower to face anything else life throws at me. Well, I will see very shortly.

So privately in a very public way, Toni, I love you.

If it takes a thousand lifetimes, my search for you will never cease, I swear I will find you.

Once again, I have read a vast amount of poetry over my now 62+ years of life. If I have reproduced a line or verse, it has not been intentional. I hope you all enjoy my fifth and final book of poetry.

Heart and soul of me

Now my days have darkened
But, she put up a hell of a fight
And tried to instil into me
To always look to the light

I can look back and smile
At the joyous fun and laughs
The happy times we spent
The love, the jokes, the gaffs

My heart is heavy and sad
My brain cannot compute
The love we hold for each other
Was never in dispute

She wouldn't let me see her
Or watch her fade away
She said, you've already seen too much
And said, away you must stay

The bravery she displayed
The strength of will inside
Made me feel honoured
She would have been my bride

But now I say goodbye
In my words of poetry
Know she will always abide
Within the heart and soul of me

Acknowledgements

To all the medical teams (doctors, nurses, counsellors, psychiatrists and reception staff) and my family and friends who continue to support and help with my ongoing recovery, thank you all so very, very much. A very special thank you to Doctor Aikaterini Nikoli and the staff at Hospital of Kos, and the wonderful Evgenia (Jenny) Bountou (Cleopatra Hotels Group) for their fast reactions and calmness when I was in need this summer (2021). My friends old and new on the beautiful islands of Menorca and Kos, without some of whom this book would not be complete. I look forward to seeing you in the summer, guys. A big thank you for your help and on certain occasions hindrance (Mark and a certain famous actress, ha-ha).

It was my mother's eightieth in June '21 and my brother Tommy wrote a piece from all the brothers. It's called To A Special Mum. It's not a poem but very apt for our mother. Tommy will retain the copyright for his piece but have no claim over the book (*Warrior Angel*).

In keeping with me trying to help young aspiring poets, there are some poems written by my great niece, Faith Goodwin, age 11 years. Faith will retain the copyright for her poems but will have no claim over the book (*Warrior Angel*).

I wish you all well and I truly hope you all enjoy my last book of poetry.

To A Special Mum

As it's your 80th birthday today, I would like to say a few words on behalf of us all.

Myself, and my brothers I'm sure, find it hard just to stand up and speak about you, because to speak about you means we have to think about your life and we know your life when we were young was very hard, and it can be quite upsetting to look back on the difficult time you had.

As older adults with grown-up families of our own we understand even more how hard it must have been for you to be left with seven children to bring up alone when not even thirty years old yourself.

It's thanks to your strength and courage that you managed to go on year after year looking after us and always putting yourself last. You deserve much more than the hand life dealt you. You deserved a husband who would stand by you, look after you and cherish you and it saddens us all this was never to be.

The way you brought us up makes us who we are today. The one thing your sons have in common is that we are all devoted husbands and family men who treat their wives with the affection and devotion you missed out on.

You brought us up this way. Our happy family lives are not a coincidence, it's a direct result of your input as a fantastic parent.

I hope we have all inherited your caring nature, your huge heart and unwavering sense of family values.

You are such a special person and we all love you

so much so happy birthday today and many, many happy returns with much love from us all.

YOUR BOYS
 XXX

Written by Thomas Kevan Goodwin who also retains the copyright for speech.

1

Warrior Angel

There'll be another warrior angel
Soon, up above
She's taking with her, my heart and soul
And every ounce of love

I can see her wings forming
While she suffers through the pain
She saved my life over and over
And stopped my going insane

They say he takes the good ones
Early to his flock
But there's no reason to make her suffer
As she races against the clock

I want to make it through Christmas
So, I'll fight with all I've got
She said to me quite recently.
Cos ready to go I'm not.

With her right now I'd swap places
In an instant, without a thought
I'd gladly trade her for me
For all the love she's brought

But we all know, that can't happen
So, I'll cage my tears and rage
And watch her smile so sweetly
As she approaches the final stage

Her grace, her warmth, her goodness
In my heart will always dwell
And I will always love her
As I walk alone, through this living hell

2

For Eternity, Forever

Life is a constant battle
I've faced it, I've fought
There's nothing left to hurt me
Or that's what I thought

I've been beaten and had bones broken
Mentally and physically abused
Baseball battered, shot at, stabbed
And had my intelligence used

Sworn at, spat at, downtrodden
Hospitalised and been on the news
Twice they sent me to heaven
But entry, I was refused

So, there's no more pain
Anyone, could bring to my demise
No! Once again I'm mistaken
What an awful surprise

They're taking my angel from me
Filled me with horror and dread
There's nothing I can do to help her
Cancer right through they said

So now, I watch her wings forming
As the pain, she tries to disguise
How I wish, I could swap places
You can still see the love in her eyes

She said she'll watch over me
And come visit when she can
Doesn't matter what happens
For eternity I'll be her man

The strength and the will inside her
Makes me proud in a weird way
She's much braver than I am
Forever I'll love you Toni Grey

3

Sometimes Wonder

I've really had enough
I'm happy but mostly sad
The memories I have
Some happy but mostly bad

They frequently pay a visit
In the day but mostly night
Burning dark visions
About the life, I've had to fight

I've already been through it
Fought and lost some
Not happy with the person
My mind says I've become

Stuck in constant battle
I fight inside my head
Perhaps it would have been better
If I'd have lost and died instead

Why do I do it
Continue to fight in my mind
Relentless haunting memories
To which I wish, I was blind?

Inside, I made a decision
I had to stay and fight
But I often wonder
If my decision, was right

4

Turmoil

You really have no idea
It's impossible to explain
The fight I have inside me
When trying not to empty my veins

The battle I have in my mind
Goes on throughout the day
The flashbacks and the nightmares
Internally screaming the night away

Sitting with knife in hand
Pointed at wrist, to lacerate
Waiting for a decision
Whilst my mind, is in debate

Trying to find a reason
Not to take my life
Confusion, depression, devastation
Turmoil is running rife

Should I go, or should I stay?
Not knowing what to do
What will be the decision?
I haven't got a clue

5

Vain

They wrote a poem about me
I could tell what they had in mind
Especially when they were saying
Modest, caring and kind

I got quite a buzz
Reading it, you know
Got quite embarrassed
My face a reddish glow

When they said that bit
About helping the weak
Standing up to tyranny
Speaking for those, who could not speak

I felt quite elated
Head up in the air
Shoulders squared, chest puffed out
Like on a parade square

It went on and on
About the deeds that were performed
Helpful, powerful, unrelenting
Never bowed or conformed

It was then I realised
As the next verse, I did see
Loving, loyal, truthful
Oh fuck! It's definitely not me

6

Dragon Proposal

She has a silver dragon
A diamond it does hold
I went to see the ink master
Who turned silver to gold

It's a beautiful diamond
I took it from her hand
Gave it to a jeweller
To put it in a band

Now an engagement ring it formed
In its band of gold
Gleaming, sparkling, shining
A beautiful sight to behold

I wrote some poems for you
My heart bled on the pages
My soul has searched for you
As it battled through the ages

You know my heart is not whole
But I've found the other part
It's sitting there in your hand
It's been there from the start

So now I kneel before you
And ask for all to see
Will you make my heart whole?
Will you marry me?

7

Stand, My Love

I asked again
And wanted to say,
Don't care what's left
Marry me today.

This time, she paused
And with a twinkle in her eye
Said there's not much time
You know, I'm going to die

I said I know
The cancer won't wait
You can wear my ring
Passing through heaven's gate

She smiled at me softly
And said with pride
My only regret
Is I'm not your bride.

I said, I can fix that
Right here, right now
Put on this diamond
And this I vow

I will search for you
Until the end of time
I swear I'll find you
And make you mine

This time the poem
I read from my heart
Tears in my eyes
As I spoke the last part

She looked at me sweetly
I was down on one knee
She said, stand, my love
You're engaged to me

8

Bad Place

Sorry I've been missing
I've travelled through my mind
Thanks for keeping your distance
I'm not pleasant at times, you'll find

Been in a really bad place
Trapped inside my head
Fighting through bad memories
Talking to the dead

Not one to express bad feelings
I lock them up inside
But sometimes they explode
Good and bad memories collide

Pull yourself together
Well, don't you think I've tried?
The darkness descends upon me
There's no place I can hide

Things I've seen and done
Some not very nice
Unless you've walked in my shoes
Don't bother with your advice

It's a battle I have to face
Sometimes every day
Because, what's inside me
Will never go away

So, I'll fight to keep the goodness
And try to banish the bad
Then, I can resume living
The good life I once had

Thank you for the good wishes
And the birthday greets I had
But I have to keep my distance
It prevents me going mad

I know some people love me
And a big thank you to those
It helps me keep on fighting
When nightmares and flashbacks impose

9

Reaper's Afraid of Me

Death has touched me more than once
It follows me around
Started when I was very young
The time I nearly drowned

You see his pointed fingers
Always head for me
The reaper with his cycle
Trying to set my soul free

I've seen my comrades fall
Loved ones slowly die
Even childhood friends
Taken by, the catcher in the rye

I guess it's not so long
The length of a life
So, enjoy it while you can
Forget the stress and strife

So when he comes calling
Says, a place for you, he's made
You can walk the path
As your light begins to fade

I'm waiting for him to call
More than twice, he's been to see
If I'm ready to go
But the reaper is afraid of me

So, I'll watch them fall
Loved ones, friends, family
I think he only takes them
Just to torture me

10

At This Gate

So, I awoke at two a.m.
I had to write a poem
Repeating over and over
My mind would not leave me alone

I had created a picture
Me, a dark angel, was empowered
I carried a white angel
As her life's light was devoured

Flying upwards slowly
To arrive at heaven's gate
She turned and spoke quite softly
For you right here, I'll wait.

No! I said quite sternly
You must go into the light
For me to enter that place
Will be a lengthy fight

I'll never be allowed in there
For all I've done in the past
No saintly ring above me
My demons, out, I cannot cast

The wicked boy that I was
I've fought and killed and maimed
The reaper is afraid of me
On the dark side, I have trained

Oh no my love, she told me
For all your past sins you have paid
You've helped save and build some families
A new path you have paved

I can't change my past
Or the bad deeds I have done
They'll never allow me in there
No matter how good or bright I've shone

Listen, she said softly
And have a little faith
You've saved a lot of people
From arriving early, at heaven's gate

I can see your black wings
Getting lighter every day
She said, I'll be waiting for you
So at this gate I'll stay

Kos 2020

11

Remember It for Life

Sitting early evening
At Alma restaurant, here in Kos
There's always something happening
You're never at a loss

I could hear people start cheering
Clapping and whooping getting close
What the hell is happening?
I quickly asked the host

A parade of some sort, well, maybe
But not normal this time of year
Louder, louder, louder
Clapping and cheering getting near

I stood and walked to the entrance
So I could see what there was to see
Other people in the restaurant
Standing and joining me

Just then they pass us
Smiling holding hands
Waving saying thank you
To the people who all stand

Looking very radiant
In a wonderful flowing dress
Her man in a kilt
Shirt neatly pressed

As they walked along
It was like a Mexican wave
Each beach restaurant they passed
Stood clapping and shouting hooray

What a wonderful experience
For the young man and new wife
Walking through Kardemena
They'll remember it for life

12

Meeting Danii

I met a girl called Danii
And Lucas was her guy
They were impressed by my story
And how I wouldn't die

It was the barman Jimi
Who told the story of me
And how it aided my recovery
To write poetry

I didn't get to speak
Or know them for long
But they were interested
In how I stood so strong

I gifted her my books
So my poetry she could read
And on the pages before her
In verse my heart did bleed

I hope she did enjoy
My books of rhyme and verse
Small segments of my life
In this lonely universe

13

Expert Waiter Michael

Having dinner at a restaurant
Almost in the sea
With the waves crashing
And the moon shining down on me

Alma is the name of the restaurant
In Kardamena Kos
The food is really good
No wastage and no loss

A dashing-looking waiter
Michael is his name
I watch as he serves his customers
Chatting as he entertains

Everybody's happy
He's serving up a treat
Dashing about quite nimbly
As his public enjoy what they eat

He'll be back tomorrow
Even if his feet are sore
Serving up a treat
At the Alma by the shore

14

The Alma Staff

Michael, Stam, Spiro, Maria

You inspire me with your ethic
I like to watch you work
Nothing is too much trouble
You never go berserk

With a troublesome customer
Your manner is polite
Never lose your cool
Even when they want to fight

Some are fuelled with alcohol
And there's trouble in the air
You calm them down with kindness
You treat them very fair

Your responsibility is vast
For everyone you care
All enjoying their evening
With your culinary fare

All through the season
Without a proper thanks
You feed the hungry holidayers
Who don't give a second glance

They're here and then they're gone
Back to their normal life
And you can be quite proud
You've provided for your children and your wife

15

Love's Mystical Dream

The evening brings tranquillity
As the sun slowly dies
Bringing in the darkness
Of the night's clear skies

Forming in the distance
The stars begin to shine
Lights glinting lightly
A magical evening time

The music from the restaurant
Gently breaks the silence
Crashing with obeyance
A rhythmic flow and a beautiful scene

Hand in hand, the lover's dream
Watching from a distance, their hearts beat in time
They'll be together forever
Love's mystical rhyme

16

Quite Amazing

How do they do it?
Balance, movement, poise
Passing through the tables
No bangs or clattering noise

I think it's quite amazing
To watch them all be fed
A dozen plates in their arms
Waiters never lose their heads

I see it time and time again
Their balance is supreme
Holidayers fed
And still plenty of plates to clean

I couldn't do it
Wouldn't know where to start
I'd be passing out dinners
From a horse and cart

17

Alma Restaurant Front Line

Maria, Spiro, Michael
The dynamic duo plus one
Smoothly move between tables
Until service is all done

Taking orders, feeding, cleaning
Until everyone is full
Always smiling happily
Enjoying all the fun

Working very hard
So everyone enjoys
The evening's entertainment
The songs, the laughter, the noise

After everything is done
And the restaurant can close
They can relax until tomorrow
Because on and on the summer goes

When it's time to rest
And the season is all done
They can have their holiday
And wait for the next season to come

18

Bullshit

I don't need to speak
I just have to listen
Operating your mouth loud
You don't know what you're missing

When you don't talk
It's amazing what you hear
The cackling I've found
Comes out a lot with beer

Sometimes not even loud
But, stop themselves, they cannot
When tonsils are well oiled
From spilling bullshit a lot

19

Sunrise on a Horse

I wanted to go horse riding
I'd never been before
I spotted early morning
It's the sunrise on the shore

Feeling apprehensive, I looked
And booked the ride
Then I booked an evening one
Same day so I couldn't hide

So early in the morning
Outside Cleopatra superior hotel
George came and picked me up
There was another couple as well

When we arrived at the stables
Monica was there to greet
And explain to us how to mount
And position head, hands and feet

I was on a wonderful horse
His manner was extremely good
If he decided to lose me
I'm very sure he could

Monica walked alongside me
I really felt great
Riding this magnificent animal
But going at his pace

Going toward the beach
Seeing the islands in the distance
Tranquillity and bliss
What a wonderful existence

Riding along the sand
Quite close to the sea
The sun starting to emerge
On the horizon, wonderfully

Well I must say
What a feeling, what a sight
Monica took some pictures
Kardamena horse riding, pure delight

20

Pirate Prince

We're going on a cruise
The three-island tour
Well it's something new
I've never been before

I have got to get to the harbour
For which they provide a bus
There were some children on there
Causing quite a fuss

Parents trying to control them
But you could see the excitement there
We're going on a pirate ship
In the Black Pearl's captain's care

So, we set off
On this three-island tour
Chatting as we sailed
Stops, there would be four

Chatting with some Dutch girls
About my poetry
Then a Dutchman piped up
Well write a poem for me

Just then as we were talking
On the rigging up above
Oh no there's a madman
Swinging from the yard arm, my love

Up and down the rigging
Dangling from the sails
Dancing on the deck
Running alone the rails

Losing his balance
Slipping over the side
Swinging back with a rope
Into the captain he did collide

We thought, oh! He's in trouble
Here comes the bosun's mate
Then they decide to tell us
He's part of the crew. That's great

On his first performance
He had us all convinced
That he was just a madman
But he's really a pirate prince

So even without the islands
And the swimming by the shore
It was a really great excursion
I'm coming back for more

21

Scaring All the Children

If you see a pirate
On a pirate ship
Swinging through the rigging
Cutlass attached to hip

Be careful when he's passing
A ransom he may want
Sending you a kidnapper note
In a very ancient font

He's fighting with his cutlass
Charging around the deck
Tripping and slipping
Oops he nearly broke his neck

Scaring all the children
They are screaming and laughing loud
A couple draw swords to fight him
Their parents are very proud

Taking lots of photos
Of their children on the cruise
The three-island tour
Is a great day out to choose

22

Kardamena Mountain Ride

Having already been once
I'm waiting for George to arrive
For my mountain evening ride
He will pick me up at five

I so enjoyed it this morning
My first time on a horse
If I had known how exhilarating it was
I would have done it earlier, of course

Monica was there to greet us
And again explain her plan
To take us up the mountain
And down, as safely as she can

Again she walked beside me
Up the mountain path
The views were so amazing
And the conversation a great laugh

What an amazing couple
George and Monica are
Horse riding in Kardamena
Is the best thing, by far

If you're in Kardamena
Holidaying by the sea
Book a ride with Monica
It's amazing, I think you'll agree

23

Kardamena 2020

All dealing with covid
In their own particular way
The staff at Cleopatra Superior
Were all marvellous I must say

Maria on reception
Would always find the time
To explain what you needed to know
Even translate a sign

Joanna was another
She was exactly the same
I'm pretty sure she told me
It was from Australia she came

Jimi at the pool bar
Was always up for a chat
What a nice personality
Knew a lot about this and that

Leonora was from housekeeping
We couldn't exchange a word
But my room was always spotless
And everything neatly prepared

Boss lady Jenny
Never had no fuss
Efficiently controlling
Three hotels for us

Controlling restaurant Alma
Sitting by the sea
Cleopatra Superior
Hotel Cleopatra and Kris Mari

Looking for a holiday
Well trust me
Nowhere else is better
Than Kardamena in Kos, go see

24

Footprints in the Snow

Poem written by Faith Danielle Goodwin, age 11
years.

Across the field there's footprints
From bunnies in the snow
In the field a snowman
Or a snow covered scarecrow

So bright and yet so cold
Oh so beautiful the sight
Snow covered fields and roof tops
All glistening white

It's really cold today
The frost is far and wide
But looking at this picture
Makes me feel all warm inside

25

Lifetime You Had

You need fuel to light a fire
Bringing energy from within
Memories are the flames
Of the good, the bad and the sin

You really need to feel
All the emotion inside
The bad and the good
As your memoires collide

Could start off happy
And end up sad
An entanglement of emotion
Is the lifetime you've had

Shall I start here?
No, where to begin?
A torrent of torment
The thoughts you hold within

The beaming rays of happiness
Of which you played a part
Memories of a kind nature
There, could be your start

A lifetime of health and wealth
Is a story to tell
Well I guess I'll think about it
While I wallow here in hell

26

I'll take it from you

I'd take your sickness from you
Your pain and all the rest
I wish I could have everything that ails you
So you could be at your best

No trail or tribulation
I would ever shirk
All the bad things that happen
I'd take them from your earth

Your world would be at its best
No pain or illness there
I would accept everything
And wouldn't really care

To see you pain free and happy
Is all I'd ever want for you
I would take all the bad things
For you, my love, so true

27

Eternal Bliss

If I can make you happy
Even, just for a bit
I'd scrimp and scrape, bow and break
And wallow in pig shit

Anything I could do
To brighten up your day
I would gladly do
You don't even have to say

To see a bright tomorrow
Banish all the bad
I would give up everything
And still be happy and glad

Glad to see the person
Beaming smile upon her face
Who's been to hell and back
And your sadness, I'll replace

And to avoid confusion
Just remember this
My love for you is eternal
Your happiness is my bliss

28

Repair Your Unicorn

Ride in your dreams on magical beings
Your heart will be reborn
Soaring high through the sky
Flying your magical unicorn

Flying away from troubled past
Gliding smoothly through the sky
Making dreams, flying so fast
Your heart will mend and no longer cry

Dreams may only be in your head
But, so is the destruction
The devastation and the dread
Can lead to reconstruction

So in your dreams
Make happy and bright
Defeat the badness
And turn to the light

See yourself soaring way up high
Gliding gently, letting the past lie
Know your heart is not forlorn
It will repair with your inner unicorn

29

Should I Have

In the prison of my mind
The light seems to fade
Ghouls and demons float around
As bad memories parade

Should I have done this or that?
Was I right or wrong?
As I question decisions from my past
As the memories linger on

Should I have taken another path
And waited a minute or two?
Should I have got closer
I may have obtained a clearer view

Should I have put greater distance
Between me and you?
Then, maybe I wouldn't care
What I did or didn't do

30

Turn Live Around

Whatever way you live
There evil can be found
We don't aspire to it
But sometimes turn live around

Strange how four letters
Can mean such different things
Around you have to turn it
And see which one it brings

I suppose some are both
They live an evil life
They just enjoy the worry
The trouble, the stress, the strife

Some are just pure evil
They enjoy the wicked side
Can't stand to see people happy
Goodness and enjoyment, they can't abide

Some they choose to live
With, what will be, will be
Try make people happy
Enjoyment they like to see

Bouncing back from trouble
Bouncing back from depressive clouds
There's always a way to deal with it
And turn that evil word around

31

At College

Well thank you Mrs Teacher
Alexis has done so well
Settled in so quickly
And even learnt to spell

She's happy in your classroom
And learning is a joy
Your talent and your kindness
Educating a girl or boy

So just to say thank you
For your patience and your knowledge
I'll bet Alexis remembers you
Even when she's at college

32

Just Because They Can

I went to see the judge
She was really quite nice
Didn't listen to the morons
And took my doctor's advice

So, now I'm sitting pretty
Well, I can afford to eat
And when I get my money
I'll be back on my feet

It's not going to be easy
But, I think I'll get by
With financial assistance
I can cook and eat a pie

No more going to the food bank
No more begging and pleading for help
No more crying in the corner
And letting out a little yelp

I can go and buy food
I can cook it in a pan
It's terrible what they can do to you
Just because they can

33

I Fuckin' Wish

Ha! Ha!

You look like Jason Statham
No! I disagree
Yes! You certainly look like Statham
No! I don't, trust me

Do you think he looks like Jason?
Oh! Yes I do agree
He's definitely got a look of him
From certain angle, I can see

You look like Jason Statham
No! I don't think I do
We definitely think you look alike
Well, that's just the opinion of you two

I don't look like Statham
And I'll tell you why
Because I was born before him
So, he must look like I

Menorca 2021

An absolutely magical island. It stole my heart twenty years ago and has not lost any of its attraction to me at any stage. The people are so generous and friendly, I have a lot of friends there, and will always return while I'm able.

34

Tranquillity and Grace

Here I am again
In Menorca, I'm happy to be
Seeing some old friends
In a restaurant by the sea

Mirador front line staff
Are obviously not the same
I only know two
I think covid is to blame

Owner Tony is obviously here
Stalwart Iona is still in the crew
In fact I don't know what Tony
Without Iona would do

Busy time again
For all the staff
I'm happy to see they're working
Enjoying and having a laugh

Must have been really difficult
No customers, because Covid was here
Pretty awful for everyone
Trying to get through last year

But it's nice to see the smile
Coming back to this place
Where holidaymakers enjoy
The beauty of tranquillity and grace

35

O'Malley's the Start

This new bar O'Malley's
Is really full of fun
New owner Kenny
Can be proud of what he's done

First I met in there Paul
He's Kenny's mate
Introduced to Mark and Michelle
And they were great

The girls then did appear
I call them the British three
Maureen, Mim and Linda
With them, it was great to be

So we formed a gang of six
Laughing joking having fun
I think everyone enjoyed it
And new friendships have begun

Other holidaymakers called in
And joined our noisy crowd
We had a few complaints
Not to be so loud

But we just turned up the music
To smother our din
And all the people moaning
Eventually joined in

So happiness was had
No drunkenness or brawls
So, when in Arenal
To O'Malley's, everyone calls

36

Finish Off the Night

Meeting Mark and Michelle
At a restaurant by the sea
But I forgot
Which one could it be?

I know, I'll go to O'Malley's
I guess that's where they'll start
After three or four
I thought, I'd best depart

So, to Mirador I went
It's my favourite place to eat
I have to have food before I drink
Or I'll be staggering down the street

Eventually they arrive
Said, we knew you'd be here
While you finish your food
We'll sit and have a beer

Up to O'Malley's we went
To finish off the night
It was really pretty quiet
Something wasn't right

But within a few minutes
Everything was bright
Diane had brought the British three
To everyone's delight

37

The British Three

You've heard of Charlie's Angels
Well, what about the British three?
Mim, Maureen, Linda
Superstars they should be

Mim is a local councillor
But not when she goes abroad
She becomes a dancing angel
And is not to be ignored

She'll choose a selection of music
And spin around the floor
Leaving other holidaymakers
Shouting more, more, more

Maureen's a racehorse owner
She had a famous win
But her horse is in the stable
When holidays begin

She'll laugh and scream and giggle
When the dancing does begin
Even draws a crowd
As around the floor she'll spin

Linda is a receptionist
Of her job she's very proud
But always hits the dance floor
When the music is playing loud

She'll stand and leave her table
And shimmy through the crowd
Spinning, turning, grooving
Looking really proud

Great fun are these three angels
An atmosphere they create
We sit and wait at O'Malley's
Me, Mark and Michelle my mates

O'Malley's is now open
A new bar for us to meet
Ken is the owner
He's usually rushed off his feet

The evenings are always famous
As for, The British Three we wait
Dancing, singing, laughing
On a holiday they made great

38

Orlando's Tenth Encore

I met a brilliant artist
In Arenal d'en Castell
The guy was a fantastic singer
From him to the real artists you couldn't tell

We were walking up from the beach
The sun was going down
Then we saw a notice
Orlando is here in town

At the five o one
We entered and took our seats
It was getting pretty busy
As out, the music gently beats

Then came on our artist
We hadn't seen him before
But soon his dulcet tones
Had us clamouring for more

He was quite an entertainer
With a magical melodic voice
We wanted more, more, more
And left him with no choice

By the time he finished his set
With the music that he sings
The crowd was growing larger
Because of the happiness he brings

His singing was so good
So, for an encore we did yell
Captivating his audience
Pulling us all under his spell

People now up dancing
Enjoying every song
Partying like no tomorrow
Orlando deserves a gong

Eventually that's it
He said, I've got no more
Thank you for this evening
I enjoyed my tenth encore

39

The Hostess with the Mostest

This is just to thank you
From the bottom of my heart
Without your help and guidance
I wouldn't know where to start

If I get the bus
I'll ask Claudia at what time
She will give me a timetable
And everything will be fine

Wanted to book some trips
So I went and asked my mate
She said, I'm really sorry
You've left it far too late.

So we'll meet up for lunch
For half an hour or so
I'm sure the time will pass real fast
Cos' back to work, Claudia must go

Sitting chatting happily
Slowly eating lunch
Sipping at our beer
The salad has a crispy crunch

Chatting about our past times
And some fun we once had
Mixing the conversation
To also include the bad

Pleasantries and memories
Make the conversation flow
But, oh my God look at the time
Claudia now must go

Well I've had a super hour
It's really passed so fast
Thank you for the new memory
And a friendship I hope will last

40

Secret Codes

There is a secret code
Between them I'm sure
Definitely three restaurants
Maybe even four

I'm starting to watch
The signals, I'll work it out
There is communication
Of that, there is no doubt

First one is good
It's the single right arm
Waving up above you
Means there's no harm

It means good customer
On the way
Pleasant, cheerful, kind
And they always pay

The second I've noticed, once or twice
Left arm held up, forming a stop
Right arm waving stopping at left
Means one customer is pretty bereft

The third I've noticed, causing alarm
Both arms waving forming an X
It's not the X-Factor on TV
It's to tell you they're vexed you see

They'll come in, they'll insult you
They'll shout and scream and perform
They won't apologise for any of their lies
To them it's just the norm

So, beware if you get the third signal
Don't let them in
They'll curse and fuss until you combust
And the havoc will soon begin

Mysterious Beauty One, Two, Three

I'm looking for an angel
A beauty I once saw
I couldn't look last year
Covid closed this shore

So now two years later
I'm in Arenal
Looking for the mysterious one
So I can show and tell

Two years ago I saw her
I wrote for you a poem
You said you enjoyed it
But to me you were unknown

Mysterious beauty
Was a poem I wrote
I put it in my book
With other poems of note

In the Menorcan section
Of my last book
Bad or Good Face It
Have it, take a look

I walked into a restaurant
And guess who I saw
Little mysterious beauty
Moving toward me across the floor

I wrote a poem for you.
Yes! She said, you did,
You made my day for me
I was as happy as a kid

So now I have another surprise
Producing a book from my bag
Her eyes lit up and a beaming smile
She knew it was no blag

Going to the page
Mysterious beauty was there
Bold print on a page
Looking straight at her

Oh! My God, she said
You've made my day again
As I signed the book
Her happiness, she could not contain

Well now I wrote this poem
And on new pages it will be
If I find you in the summer
I can make your day again, see

42

Lockdown Through a Child's Eyes

Poem written by Faith Danielle Goodwin, aged 11
years.

Adults surround us
All wearing masks
We've heard them talk about it
But we're too scared to ask

What is this virus
That they're all speaking about?
It's all over the news
Why can't we just stamp it out?

Mum's working from home now
It's really quite nice
Though I'm frightened to catch this virus
Once maybe even twice

Sent home from school
Work to do at home
But we're better off than most
So I really can't moan

Not allowed to see
Our family or friends
It feels like this nightmare
Is never going to end

Please think of us children
When you're out and about
Please slip down your mask
And smile to help ease our doubt

It's really quite scary
When you're little like me
You seem to feel like
Your living an old scene from ET

43

Everything Stops for the DWP

Well excuse me Mr Doctor
If I may be so bold
The benefits office needs a letter
So, put intensive care on hold

You, have to stop what you're doing
Although its vital work
The benefits office won't pay me
And I may go berserk

I have a brain injury
That will never heal
A heart monitor in my chest
So the rhythm it can reveal

I have diabetes
And arthritis running rife
Blackouts are common
The domestic abuse changed my life

My GP, brain and heart consultants
Say, I'll never work again
But, some bright spark in the DWP
Says I'm fit for work and then

They're stopping my benefit
Cos, I told them, there's been no change
So, I guess I'll have to wait another year
Until a court date can be arranged

These people have no idea
What trauma they put me through
The only thing in my life that's stable
Is the benefit I'm entitled to

So, when they send you a form
And tell you fill it in
It's just time they're wasting
I'm sure it goes in the bin

With the brain injury I need assistance
So, other people I annoy
Get them to do it for me
Like a baby or toddling boy

Don't they know I have pride
Worked all my life since a boy?
And then on top of Christmas
Once again, my life, they destroy

I want to go back to work
But, the physicians say, no joy.
You'll never work again
Your ailments are not a ploy.

So, now I have to beg
For assistance, it's no life
No wonder PTSD suicide
Is absolutely rife

I wish they'd let me try
Put back some meaning to my life
But no! I'm only a statistic
Of a man almost killed, by a wife

44

Manslaughter

Am I not in my right mind
Sorry, is it just me?
Is it not wrong for an eighty year old
To visit a hospital, for a friend to see?

In this environment
Covid running rife
Operations delayed
Except to save a life

So, if you found your mother
Who is vulnerable, you see
Was invited to attend hospital
Where Covid is running free

Would you not be angry
At the people who arranged
For your eighty-year-old mother
To stand on a shooting range?

Well, I'm fuckin' blazing
My rage is so immense
To send my mother to infection
While they're sitting on a fence

She's just so kind and vulnerable
Very stupid at times
Easily lead by morons
Who know how to hide their crimes

Yes, I look at it as criminal
Manslaughter in a sense
Leading her into Covid
Has to be a criminal offence

They don't care what happens
As long as they're not there
My mother could die tomorrow
And they just wouldn't care

So, to the hospital I must take her
She's as stubborn as a mule
And if I don't take her
It'll be some other bloody fool

So I'm fucking disgusted
Don't know what else to say
Except if she gets infected
There'll be fuckin' hell to pay

45

All Because of One

You say you haven't got it
So let me try explain
You could be the killer of thousands
Because of your selfish distain

You want to go and visit
But that's now, against the law
You think it doesn't apply to you
You been doing it for fifteen years or more

But now in a dangerous environment
You are vulnerable as well
A member of your household
Tends the sick, but can't break the spell

So, maybe they give it to you
And you may not even know
Then you visit your friend
And pass the disease so it can grow

Your friend has a visit from her son
Who's then infected but can't tell
So when he sees his daughter
She is now infected as well

His daughter has a partner
She shares infection with him
They both infect their child
But there's no sign of infection within

The partner infects his mother
Who infects her partner and siblings
They go off to school
And a new pandemic begins

Can you see where this is going?
Each with a meeting of one
Thousands now infected
Because of what one has done

The rules are there for a reason
Breaking them is not great fun
Thousands are ill and dying
Because you wanted to visit just one

46

Steadfast and True

Eileen my neighbour
Steadfast and true
Caring and honest
She'll always help you through

Confide in her your pain
All your sad thoughts
She'll listen with compassion
A confidante of sorts

Always a kind word
And always happy to see
A neighbour or a friend
Could be, a he or a she

When you're at your worst
And your sadness she can see
Always calm words
Kind and courteous to me

I'm glad I have a friend
In my little community
Eileen my kind friend
Who I'm always happy to see

Marvellous Dentist

Pretty ashamed of my mouth
My teeth are pretty bad
Kicked out and broken
From a beating I once had

Eventually I went the dentist
Because I wouldn't smile
Janet, took some bits out
In a calm and caring style

She said, you'll have to come back
So, I can repair your grin
We'll have to take the top ones out
And put a palette in.

I'm going for the double
Going to take them two in one
Then with a flick of her wrist
The two front ones were gone

Putting the new ones in there
She said, they may hurt for a bit
But when the pain has receded
Your cheeky smile will match your wit

So, thank you marvellous dentist
For the smile you gave back to me
Now, I can laugh
At the funny things I see

48

Crafty Poppy the Puppy

Yippee we're going away on holiday
Everyone is jumping for joy
I don't know what a holiday is
Because I'm not a girl or a boy

I'm Poppy the puppy
I'm really very small
When something frightens me
I curl up in a ball

Alexis is my best friend
She takes care of me
And her mummy and Lewis love me
That's plain for all to see

Poppy the puppy
Is only very small
You can hardly see her
When she curls up in a ball

She likes to follow you
And snap playfully at your feet
She'll give you a little cuddle
It's really quite a treat

When you're playing and dancing
She'll sit and watch you play
Then she'll start crying
So you pick her up, that's her ploy

49

Unicorns Can Bring

Thank you Mr Unicorn
For helping me learn art
Music and dancing
Are sewn into my heart

I like to go to classes
To learn to dance and sing
So thank you for the happiness
That only unicorns can bring

50

Soulmate (walk through hell)

It's said you'll always know
It's said you'll never part
When you find your soulmate
You can read each other's heart

It could take a thousand lifetimes
Throughout all eternity
But, you will always find them
It's written in destiny

Then no matter how far
In distance you're apart
You will always be
Inside each other's heart

I love you more than anything
In my heart you'll always dwell
I can't explain the joy you bring
For you, I'd gladly walk through hell

Crazy Brain-Damaged, Tourette's Poet

I was only fuckin' joking
I never fuckin' swear
Really though, when I'm pissed off
Blue I turn the fuckin' air

But, last night I wasn't
I knew whose car it was
I just blocked you in
So, I could swear at the fuckin' boss

She always pays attention
When I'm about
I rant and rave and cause a fuss
And generally fuck about

Sorry if I upset you
When I fuckin' swear
But I know your sister finds it funny
When blue I turn the air

52

A Lifetime Cannot Forget

Can't wait to hold you close
The feeling of skin next to skin
Look deep into your eyes
And see the love that lays within

Touch your beautiful hair
Brush my fingers down your cheek
Gently hold you near
As we find the love we seek

Our hearts and minds entwine
As we hold each other close
Whisper in your ear
You're the one I love the most

And many years from now
We'll look back with no regret
At all the wonderful memories
That a lifetime cannot forget

Kos 2021

Kos is an absolutely beautiful island. The people are very friendly, great fun to be with. They are very knowledgeable about their island and the surrounding islands. They like their food so what they serve up to you is fantastic. Everything is friendly and enjoyable. The Cleopatra Superior, The Cleopatra and The Kris Mari in Kardamena are exceptional.

53

Front Line Jen

Almost a year has passed
Since I met her once before
Just exchanged pleasantries
You know, say hello and hold open a door

This year in an emergency
She took complete control
Ordered a car for the hospital
Spoke to me, trying to console

Gave me a card with her mobile
Said, whatever you need
Call me and I'll try to help you
While I continued to bleed

At the hospital there was no problem
They sorted me out in a flash
Only four hours I was missing
Although I returned with a lot less cash

Next day I saw Jenny standing
Just by the reception desk
She said, I was just asking about you
But you can tell me now in the flesh

I told her what the hospital told me
She listened with kindness and intent
Telling me to be careful, go slowly
And off to the pharmacy I was sent

I spoke to her later that evening
Explaining in detail, a lot more
What had happened to me
And that it had happened before

Next day Jen asked, if I knew
Cleopatra Superior was closing
So by the end of the week
Go to Kris Mari, she was supposing

She said, I'll sort it all for you
You can go whenever you want to go
Just pack all your items and clothing
To save you from going to and fro.

Well wow, what had Jen done?
This is a marvellous surprise
The room was so fantastic
And the view, was a sight for sore eyes

She introduced me to the new staff
That work at the Kris Mari
Asked if I liked my new room
And the view across the sea

Introduced me to Jerry
Who controlled the whole pool area
He knew and he spoke to everyone
Although Jen was his immediate superior

Sitting by the pool bar
Having a nice coffee
Laughing and joking hilariously
Jen is always good company

It's not all fun, she works hard
Always another task to complete
She's running three hotels in the area
And a restaurant, that's no mean feat

Always time for everyone
A kind word here and there
Never looks ruffled or put upon
Coolness personified, I swear

When the summer is over and we are gone
I guess you'll have time to look back
At the kindness you showed everyone
And the finesse that some people lack

Hard work and fortitude
Will always get you the prize
So I'll write a poem in solitude
And in it, you, I will immortalise

54

Jerry the Pool Area Magician

Jerry works the pool area
At the Kris Mari
He told me, you want anything
Then just come to me.

The man, he knows everyone
And he's always joking about
He can make you believe that anyone
Is in, when they are out

Beer, coffee, light drinks
He makes them all appear
Want something to eat?
Jerry will bring it here

He's like a dancing magician
Fleeting here and there
Chatting and joking with everyone
Like the ringmaster at the fair

Making everyone happy
Laughing at their jokes
Then with a funny retort
Fun at everyone he pokes

He has a little get together
With twenty or so folks
Hires the whole of the Alma
The restaurant that almost floats

Everyone sitting and chatting
Enjoying the food there
Wining and dining majestically
Pleasant evening, without a care

Now all the attention is on Jerry
As he prepares a little speech
Will you all raise your glasses
To toast the restaurant on the beach

Food is all well eaten
Most enjoyable culinary fare
Everyone then starts drinking
Alcohol flowing rapidly, I swear

Next morning down at the pool bar
Not many soaking up the sun
Jerry looked over smiling
Said last night was really fun

I said, yes but where are the holidaymakers?
He said, they are sleeping, I guess
Last night after you left us
There was a real alcohol fest.

Wine was guzzled by the gallon
He was nearly off his feet
Alcohol, food and laughter
Were all at Jerry's treat

55

Jenny From the B

This is Jenny, she runs the residents' bar
She's a black country girl
But if you call her a brummy
Some glasses and bottles she might hurl

Jenny is full of knowledge
Ask her if you go there
She's very intelligent
And treats everyone fair

So, if you like a late drink
Don't be very loud
And she will serve you until two a.m.
Even if you're in a crowd

Discussing everything
Except Politics, Religion or War
Any other subject
She'll tell you what's the score

Music, groups and singers
She's exceptionally bright
If you ask, well who sang this?
She'll give you an answer and I bet she's right

Sitting there at the bar
With my new friend Joe
We behave gentlemanly
Or she'll tell us where to go

So we sit there chatting
Having lots of fun and games
Other people join us
Jenny remembers everyone's name

She's going home for Christmas
But not for very long
She'll miss Kardamena
Where she knows she belongs

56

Garlic Bread and Carbonara

Garlic bread and carbonara
Lemon sweet
Served up by Chara
What a delightful treat

Alma restaurant in Kardamena
Sits right on the sea
Beautiful location with beautiful food
It's certainly the place to be

I come here often
For their culinary delights
The staff are kind and courteous
On these lovely warm nights

Sea lapping on the beach
Only a couple of metres
You can put out your and reach
While you're sitting and enjoying your culinary treats

All are very friendly
They like you to enjoy
Everything about their food
Man, woman, girl or boy

57

Famous Writer

I met a famous writer
Jo is her name
She's sitting with Marie
Now that's a claim to fame

Never met a famous writer
That had published a book
Well, not unless you count
When in the mirror I look

Sitting having breakfast
In Alma restaurant by the sea
Started chatting happily
Jo, Marie and me

It really passed some time
Chatting about this and that
Speaking in novel form
It was really quite a chat

58

The Sunrise Ride Once More

I have been there once before
Horse riding at sunrise
I still remember the feeling
The tension, the nerves and the surprise

I booked it once again
On this my second visit
To an island full of surprises
In my mind, very exquisite

George came to pick me up
To the stables off we went
Monica was there with Lesley
A helping hand was her intent

Mounting at the stables
Sitting on my horse
Lesley walks beside me
She's in charge of course

Walking across the fields
On this wonderful horse
He knows where he's going
With no encouragement or force

Walking along the beach
Watching the horizon on the sea
The sun will soon be rising
What a beautiful sight to see

I really can't explain
I've tried it once before
How exhilarating it feels
Horse and man along the sea shore

It's just broke the horizon
Excitement in the group
As the sun bursts up before us
Photographing this marvellous scoop

I thought I wouldn't feel
The way I did before
But I had the same emotions
As when, last year, I first saw

Thank you Monica and George
And of course Lesley too
Keep these amazing stables going
I'll be back in 2022

59

Inviting You To Dine

Philip, Chara and Spiro
This year's Alma front line
Polite, courteous, happy
Inviting you to dine

All are a delight to speak to
Taking your order, offering wine
Nothing is too much trouble
Whatever you request is fine

If they don't have it
Then they will suggest
Something similar and sufficient
As to whatever was your request

Moving through the tables
Serving all the guests
No anger or frustration
Calmness personified, they're blessed

Clearing empty tables
Re-setting. Ready for more
There's always one available
If you've been there before

You can eat at the water's edge
In the evening, by candle light
Table for two can be set
For a lovely romantic night

60

Best Cocktails

In the evening, there is Jimi
At Cleopatra Superior pool bar
Always up for a conversation
While he producers the best cocktails by far

All the ladies in the evening
Come to see Jimi
That make me dance and shimmy

Serving and happily chatting
Always with a smile
He produces rocket fuel
Liqueur with style and guile

Looking after all his patrons
When they have had a drink
Not letting them have too much
In case to their knees they sink

As they filter away upstairs
Going to rest their head
They wave goodnight to Jimi
And off they go to bed

Only two or three left now
Jimi can relax again
Knowing that, end of season
He'll be going home, on a plane

61

Misery and Beauty

The misery and the beauty
I cannot figure out
Something inside you, is painful
I can see that, without a doubt

I sit and watch others
For inspiration I look
Your stunning figure always stops me
Sitting, standing or laying reading a book

But you always seem unhappy
I haven't seen you smile
You have a dower expression
Try to smile for a while

You look a million dollars
A sunbathing beauty in the sand
I would like to try and help you
So I hold out a friendship hand

Although you completely refuse it
I'm glad I had an effect
The poems that I told you
Brought out a smile, that was perfect

Now that I've seen it
That marvellous smile
I hope you can retain it
If only for a while

62

Riding up the Mountain

Off to our evening horse ride
George has collected us
Six of us this time
Calm and quiet, no fuss

There's myself, Gordon and Julien
Pauline, Jana and Sophia
Instructions from Monica are given
And she makes the orders clear

It was me leading off
With Gordon right behind
Ali with the two of us
To make sure the trail, we find

Sophia followed Gordon
With her mother Jana, close up next
Monica walked with Sophia
Because children Monica protects

Jana close behind
So all of the ride
She could watch her young daughter
Filled with so much pride

Julien was next
With Pauline at the rear
George walked with them
All enjoyment with no fear

I'm sure we all enjoyed
The scenery from the mountain
And I know for me, I'm sure
I will return again

63

Joe Murray Sir

Absolutely no hurry
Never in a rush
No strain upon him
Definitely no fuss

Have you met my new friend?
Joe Murray is his name
Comes from Washington
Supports Sunderland at the game

Told me a little ditty
That I just had to write
He didn't know who wrote it
I hope it's not copyright

Poor old Joe
Lost in the snow
Nowhere to wander
And nowhere to go

Don't know if it was my drunkenness
When I heard that rhyme
But I had never heard it
And I'm not claiming it to be mine

But anyway we got on well
Had a few beers while we were there
I don't show much respect for just anyone
I do for you Joe Murray, Sir

Hidden People

Reptiles and lizards
Slippery slimy snakes
When you come across them
It's hard to tell the snakes

The reptiles approach with stealth
Cautious to gain trust
Bolster your ego and pride
Gaining your confidence is a must

Lizards creep right in
Before you know it they're at your side
Stoking your ego
In plain sight they hide

Then you get the slippery snakes
Coming, them you cannot see
But they're slimy, nothing sticks
And they're always, no! It wasn't me

You think I'm talking about animals
Well I'm afraid I'm not
Be careful with your valuables
They will take the fuckin' lot

65

Christmas Dinner

This was a thank-you note to my sister-in-law, Anne.

Well I must say
That was bloody great
Pass the chef my compliments
And I'll return your empty plates

Carrot and turnip, sprouts
Peas and broad beans
Spuds, pigs in blankets, turkey
All taste supreme

It makes a lovely change
For someone to cook for me
And I truly enjoyed it
I might invite myself for tea

66

Bully

Shut up, don't talk
Don't answer back
Shut up, don't talk
I'll give you a smack

Sit down, wait there
Don't talk to him
Don't talk to anyone
Friendship is a sin

Don't do this
Don't do that
Don't do anything
As a matter of fact

Ask my permission
If you want to do
Absolutely anything
Cos' I control you

You need me, you know
You can't do without
My controlling influence
Of that there's no doubt

So, shut up and sit there
While I work everything out
You're useless without me
I'm your controlling lout

Now he's sorry he hurt you
He's sorry for what he said
You dumped the controlling bully
And you're living life instead

67

Really Really Nice

If I didn't have you
I wouldn't know what to do
I'd be so sad and lonely
Upset and always blue

You brighten up my life
Every single day
You make me very happy
With the things you have to say

Our meetings I look forward to
If only on the phone
When I think about you
I'm never really alone

I know that in the future
Together we will stay
And I can put my arms around you
Forever this way, we'll stay

I love you more than more
I've told you once or twice
You're loving, kind and gentle
And really really nice

68

He's Only Six

I'm going to a party
I think it's really great
I'm going to guzzle everything
I might end up unsteady mate

Everything that's in there
I'm going to jump right in
I'll end up staggering or falling
That's before I begin

Can't stand up in the ball pit
I fall when I'm on a slide
Cake, jelly and custard, don't agree with me
My diabetes, I'll have to hide

I'm going to get ready now
Can't miss it but don't like to mix
But he's had some brilliant parties
My grandson, he's only six

69

Pictures on My Socks

Are you nearly famous
When your picture is on your socks?
Will you be admired
When they sell them in the shops?

Are you someone special
When they put your picture there?
Someone had them made for you
With tender love and care

I was so elated
When I saw to my surprise
My picture on my socks
Could I believe my eyes?

Well I guess it's highly unusual
The gift that had been sent
My picture on my socks
What a wonderful present

Thank you to you both
What a really super gift
When I was feeling down
You've really given me a lift

70

Help to pull me through

Wings tattered and torn
Broken was my mind
Lost was all hope
Of the goodness in humankind

A long time down on my knees
No hope of a future life
Pain, torment, suffering
Demons all carried the knife

Fighting to repair
Damaged and broken mind
Trying to repair a body
Abused throughout its time

Eventually the body heals
But the mind cannot forget
The demons through the night
Fill you with regret

I now have hope inside
As my mind gets stronger yet
I can control the memories
But never will forget

I need the bad with the good
It'll help me to pull through
I have an angel with me
I'm so lucky that it's you

71

Keep Moving Forward

Life is standing still
I'm facing a brick wall
Do I, go over it or under it
Or wait for it to fall?

Moving to the left
Or moving to the right
No way around it
Do I retreat or stand and fight?

If I move backwards
It's to where I've been before
I've been, I've seen, I've done it
There's nothing new to explore

So, I guess I'll move forward
I'll stand and fight
I'll wait and rest a bit
Then make a move that's right

And if there's no way around it
I know just what I'll do
I'll summon all my strength
And plough right through

On the other side
If things don't seem bright
I'll keep moving forward
Even if I have to fight

72

Here at Home

When I'm alone
I'm not alone
I close my eyes
And feel at home

I see your smile
When you're not there
Those shining eyes
That beautiful stare

I feel your touch
Your hand in mine
I hear your voice
Inside my mind

I breathe you in
The fragrant air
I taste your lips
When you're not there

So when I'm alone
I'm not alone
Because you're in my heart
You're here at home

73

My Angelic Delight

We can climb to the heavens
Glide amongst the stars
Cruise around the cosmos
With a genuine love like ours

We can visit planet ecstasy
As our souls unite
Filled with love and passion
All the day and all the night

We could whisper, I love you
Or shout it very loud
You know that amazing feeling
When you're floating on a cloud

I would do anything
To make your dreams come true
And I'm sure you'd do the same for me
I'm so in love with you

We could cuddle together
And know it feels so right
I will always be with you
You're my angelic delight

74

Glowing Soul

I can see your glowing soul
A beautiful heart that beats within
The kindness in your face
And the strength to never give in

The compassion that you have
The elegance that you ooze
The determination to survive
When you stand against abuse

The shelter of your arms
The protection that you provide
So your children won't be harmed
The love and caring inside

Now and forevermore
And all eternity
The mother your children adore
My beautiful angel you will be

75

For you I'd cry

I wish I knew what to do
I wish I knew what to say
If I had a magic wand
I'd make your tears go away

If I could just make it right
If I could help you to get through
I'd solve your problems in an instant
If I could, I would, for you

Not good with spoken words
I can only write in verse
I wish I had it for you
But it's something you can't reverse

This probably doesn't help
But I had to try
If I could dry your tears
In exchange for you, I'd cry

76

Mentally Strong Fight

Have you ever met a fighter?
Not the physical type
So strong and mentally powerful
Ignores all the bullshit and the hype

I have, she stood alongside me
She promised to be my bride
The inner strength of my woman
Fills me with tremendous pride

Five foot and a fart
Eight stone soaking wet
Mental strength unbelievable
A person you can never forget

I watched her battle with cancer
So strong and optimistic always
The doctors said it's terminal
She said, OK, I'll fight it anyways.

I'm staying here until Christmas
I don't care what they say
I will be here when Santa
Appears on Christmas Day.

Then she set a new target
I want you to finish your book
But it's to say goodbye to you
Well, before I go, I will take a look

So, I sit and write my poetry
Now with more intensive verse
To get my manuscript to the publisher
I have to finish it first

Don't know what deadline it will be
Don't know what date to beat
But I will try to finish it
To lay it at my angel's feet

Don't know if she'll get to read it
Life really isn't fair
She doesn't need my poems to tell her
How much I really care

77

Never the Same

Heaven has called
They shouted out your name
Now our life on earth
Will never be the same

Absolutely Brilliant Individual

Had a problem with my new phone
iPhone 13 Pro
Didn't know what to do with it
Couldn't make it go

Went to the 02 shop
To get some advice
Spoke to a happy, chatty girl
Abi was very nice

She sorted everything out for me
Said, now it's all set up
Everything will transfer across
When your password you input

Couldn't remember my password
No problem, Abi sorted the device
She said, they'll get back to you
To change your password at no price

Took it home and waited
But to no avail
Tried to remember the password
But it said fail, fail, fail

Took it back to 02 the next day
Abi wasn't available there
Another girl tried to help me
And she was really good to be fair

She even spoke to the Apple man
Who gave her some advice
But still couldn't gain access
To my new mobile device

So returning the following day
To the 02 shop again
I saw Abi was present
But thought, I'm beginning to be a pain

She smiled and said
Hello how are you, is everything OK?
To which I replied, no I'm sorry
My problem hasn't gone away

I will remedy everything
I have another way
To get your old phone's information
On your new phone today

So now, happy to hear that
She took my phones away
Came back a little later
Task completed, hooray!

And now I have just written
A lovely little poem
To say thank you young lady
For fixing my bloody phone

Like to say thank you, Dianne

I seen a Scots lassie
On TikTok she sings and dances
I think she's very beautiful
But, I definitely don't fancy my chances

Her beauty is beyond fantastic
Her personality radiates through
Her eyes are so magnetic
You think she's looking at you

Expressions on her face are cogent
With the music and the words right through
She does a little shimmy
As she continues to dance and boogaloo

Her face is magnificently attractive
Her shape a majestic form
Her eyes electrically stunning
I guess from when she was born

I'm happy to see a personality
So full of joys of life
She, radiates the page, magnificently
Happiness and fun are rife

So, I'd just like to say thank you
You're an explosive happiness bomb
My stress levels diminish
When I find the pages you're on

80

Never Forgot

This will be the best
The last I'll ever write
It's saying how much I love you
And how you helped me with my fight

I've been to see the devil
I've offered him my life
Even with all my misdemeanours and things
She still wanted to be my wife

She saved me from the broken
When inside, I had nothing there
Drink and drugs, meeting out violence to thugs
No heart, no warmth, no care

It was when I first saw her
I felt a warmth, a glow
Inside my body, a heart did beat
A lot more I wanted to know

I got to ask her questions
With the conversation, I was pleased
She was so inspirational
She helped me up off my knees

I started to see things clear
In myself, she helped me believe
After all I'd been through
I saw potential in what I could achieve

I started to write her poems
And a challenge I did accept
If I could write and publish a book
A date with her I would get

Well it took a year
To complete my manuscript
But when in her hands I put it
To her knees she almost slipped

May of twenty-sixteen
I knew I'd found the one
And we are still together
In December of twenty-one

Unfortunately they got her
The bastards up above
She is only a youngster to me
Now cancer has gripped my love

But she's a real fighter
Even though win, she cannot
She will always live through me
In my heart, where she's never forgot

Little Fella's Drawings

I knew you would do that
You're a nuisance Fred
You've used all my paper
Now I have a poem in my head

I guess you didn't see it coming
My brain bursts out in verse
Reaching for some paper
But, oh no, you got there first

Drawing your lovely pictures
A road, in black and red
All the lovely visions
They all come from your head

I have to be careful, when I'm looking
In case I get it wrong
I might say, oh Transformers
And you say no, King Kong

The visions in your mind
Transferred through hand in ink
I didn't quite get the outline
Maybe I'm wrong I think

Doesn't quite look like it should do
You have a fascinating mind
So I'll pretend to like them
Not just to be kind

82

Lockdown Mouthy Cow

Absolutely fuckin' bouncing
I hardly know where to start
A mouthy little toerag
Abusing me when I went for a cart

Waiting in a queue outside Tesco
Moving slowly, until the front I did go
Lights on red so, we all stop
I turned back to get a trolley, for my shop

People carried on coming
They're in front of me now
My 80-year-old mother
At the front of the row

I passed a few people and then to my surprise
A rather large gob, tones starting to rise
ERR! Excuse me in a sarcastic voice
There's people waiting here, don't push to the front

I've been to get a trolley, I was at the front
OH! NO! You wasn't said nauseous cunt
Mouth started to accelerate before I could explain
This little fuckin' vixen was becoming a pain

Now people that know me, know I'm really quite placid
But when a so-called woman starts spilling out acid
It doesn't take much for my mental health to stress
I have a brain injury and a monitor in my chest

Now I've had enough she won't let me explain
All she wants to do is moan and complain
So now at tipping point I spill a volume of abuse
Being threatened with her boyfriend was as tight as a
noose

Go fuckin' get him, I started to roar
As I spotted security, approach from the door
So I turned to face them before they could grab
They immediately backed down and wanted to gab

I turned and said, I hope you feel proud
Picking on a pensioner in a shopping crowd
Oh! YES I am, do you want some ID?
I have a heart monitor and a brain injury

The security tried to calm me, so I told them
The injury is the emotional part
There's just no stopping me
Once I start

So I hope you're proud, whoever you were
I'm fuckin disgusted, but I guess you don't care
Just remember when you're in a crowd
Get your facts straight before opening your gob loud

It may be a veteran
Who's stood in harm's way
So idiots like you
Can say what you say

*Wish I had the bitch's name. I'd immortalise her in
humiliation.*

83

Come to Me

When needs must
The devil takes control
There's no controlling
A raging soul

When you're pushed in a corner
And there's no way out
The demons inside
Don't mess about

If there's nothing left
And your options are none
You have to do something
Or your life is gone

So I'll do it for you
And set you free
So you can go home
And then come to me

Garden Crime

Not very happy
In fact I'm very sad
People rooting through my things
Drives me fuckin' mad

I knew it was going to happen
When I went away
Just can't trust anyone
To listen to what you say

Never asked for anything
To be done, while I was gone
Except open and close my blinds
To let in a bit of sun

Some people just can't help it
They just got to have a nose
Rooting through my bungalow
Searching through my clothes

Wrecking my garden
Stealing all my pears
Taking just about anything
Even though it's not theirs

I'll have to be careful
About leaving next time
Because while I'm not there
Then we will see another crime

85

Enough, I Say

How many times can it break
Before it can't be repaired?
It takes away a piece
Every time it's broken, I've heard

I know now, my lives are few
I've already lost seven or eight
Only one left
Before I call at heaven's gate

So, do I need to find the pieces
Of a heart broken many times?
Or, will I be able to enter
When the final toll chimes?

I know I haven't paid
For the sins of my past
I think they punish my loved ones
So the pain inside me lasts

It's harder for me to watch
Knowing I cannot do a thing
Than for me to suffer
Any pain, to me they could bring

I bow my head and beg
For them to take your pain away
And give it all to me
You have suffered enough, I say

86

Last Conversation

Thank you for being you
You're a strong and loyal man
Thank you for all your help
Because when you say you can, you can

I've watched you progress
From the broken and the damaged
To rise from life's ashes
An awful lot you've managed

Slowly, step by step
Your confidence you did regain
Powerfully climbing upwards
But, you'll never be the same

Some things in life change you
You're never who you were before
Now standing tall and confident
You're better by much, much more

Kind hearted and so affectionate
Powerful and strong too
I wouldn't change you for anything
Especially after what you been through

I know that you will find me
In another time and place
Our love is so immense
So pure and full of grace

I know you've been a bad guy
No saintly ring upon your brow
But you're my perfect soulmate
We'll be together again somehow

When we met, you were broken
No heart, no humour, no course
Now you shine like a million stars
A majestic poetic force.

Printed in Poland
by Amazon Fulfillment
Poland Sp. z o.o., Wrocław

91167289R00076